I'M ALLERGIC

I'M ALLERGIC TO EGGS

By Walter LaPlante

Gareth Stevens
PUBLISHING

Please visit our website, www.garethstevens.com. For a free color catalog of all our high-quality books, call toll free 1-800-542-2595 or fax 1-877-542-2596.

Library of Congress Cataloging-in-Publication Data

Names: LaPlante, Walter, author.
Title: I'm allergic to eggs / Walter LaPlante.
Description: New York : Gareth Stevens Publishing, [2019] | Series: I'm allergic | Includes index.
Identifiers: LCCN 2018014471| ISBN 9781538229040 (library bound) | ISBN 9781538232385 (pbk.) | ISBN 9781538232392 (6 pack)
Subjects: LCSH: Food allergy in children–Juvenile literature. | Eggs as food–Juvenile literature. | Allergy–Juvenile literature.
Classification: LCC RJ386.5 .L37 2019 | DDC 616.97/5–dc23
LC record available at https://lccn.loc.gov/2018014471

Published in 2019 by
Gareth Stevens Publishing
111 East 14th Street, Suite 349
New York, NY 10003

Designer: Laura Bowen
Editor: Kate Mikoley

Photo credits: cover, p. 1 all_about_people/Shutterstock.com; p. 5 Andrey_Popov/ Shutterstock.com; p. 7 artapartment/Shutterstock.com; p. 9 Dudaeva/Shutterstock.com; p. 11 FatCamera/E+/Getty Images; p. 13 gorillaimages/Shutterstock.com; p. 15 TanyaRusanova/Shutterstock.com; p. 17 Peter Dazeley/The Images Bank/Getty Images; p. 19 IAN BODDY/Science Photo Library/Getty Images; p. 21 Bruce Laurance/ Photographer's Coice RF/Getty Images.

Printed in the United States of America

CPSIA compliance information: Batch #CW19GS: For further information contact Gareth Stevens, New York, New York at 1-800-542-2595.

CONTENTS

Boldface words appear in the glossary.

It's the Egg!

Do eggs make you want to scratch or make your tummy hurt? Egg allergies are one of the most common allergies in kids! An allergy is when the body **responds** to something commonly harmless like it would respond to something harmful.

White or Yolk?

An allergic **reaction** to eggs means the body is fighting the **protein** in the egg! Most people are allergic to the egg whites, but the yolk can cause reactions, too. An egg allergy includes eggs from chickens and often eggs from ducks, turkeys, and geese.

egg yolk

egg white

7

Awful Allergy

Egg allergies are often first seen when someone is a baby. The baby might throw up or get a **rash**. Kids and adults with egg allergies might have a runny nose or get a tummy ache after they eat eggs.

Egg allergies can cause swelling and speed up your heartbeat. Some people with egg allergies may have a very bad allergic reaction called anaphylaxis (an-uh-fuh-LAK-sis). This means they'll have trouble breathing. They need to see a doctor right away.

You'll see a special doctor to be sure eggs are causing your problems. They might do a skin test. They'll put a bit of egg **extract** on your skin and **prick** you. If the spot turns red and raised, it's likely an egg allergy.

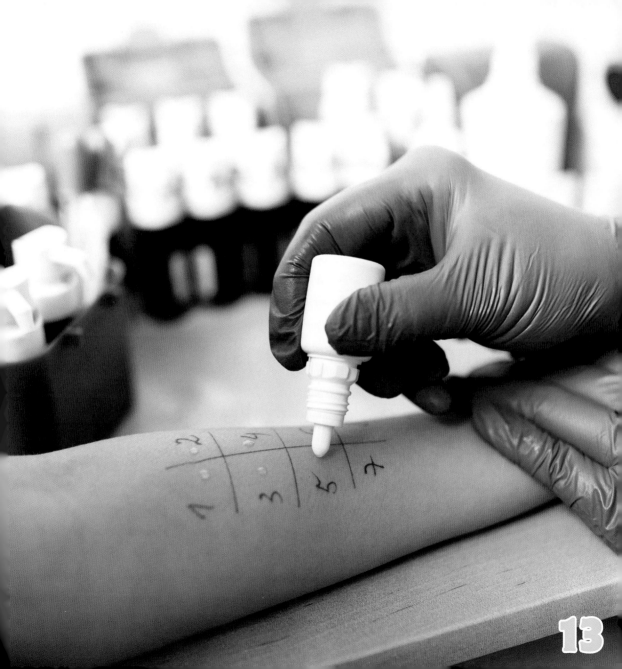

Stay Away!

The best way to stay safe with an egg allergy is to **avoid** eating all eggs! That also means not eating anything that has eggs in it. Meatloaf, cookies, cake, and even pasta often have eggs in them!

You'll need to check the **ingredients** in food to avoid eggs. Most foods with labels will say if they have eggs in them. There are also other names for eggs you'll need to check for. Make a list and carry it with you!

17

Use the Shot

Some **medicines** can help with common allergic reactions such as rashes, throwing up, or a runny nose. Someone with bad allergies needs to carry a shot filled with the medicine epinephrine (eh-puh-NEF-rihn). Someone else can give them this shot if they can't do it themselves.

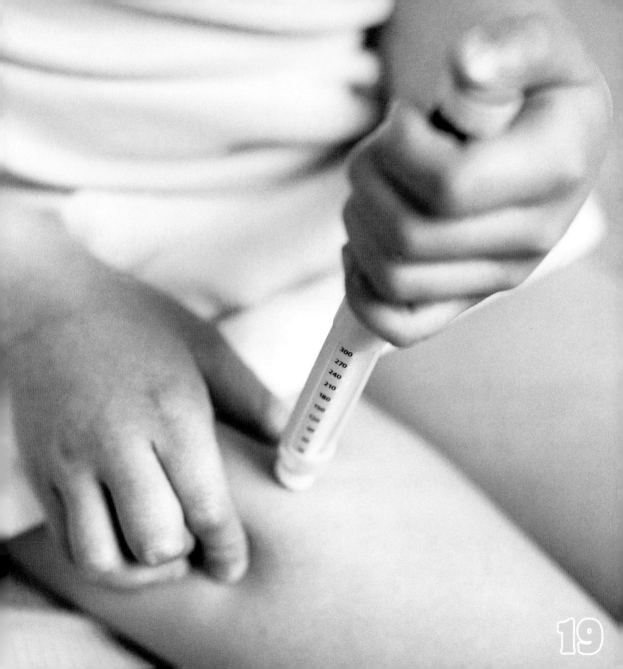

Eggs Someday?

You might get sick eating eggs today, but someday you might be able to enjoy them! Many children outgrow allergies to eggs by the time they're about 16. For now, avoiding eggs is the best thing to do!

GLOSSARY

avoid: to stay away from

extract: matter you pull out from something using a machine

ingredient: one of the things used to make food

medicine: a drug taken to make a sick person well

prick: to make a very small hole in something

protein: a necessary element found in all living things

rash: a group of red spots on the skin

reaction: the way your body acts because of certain matter or surroundings

respond: to do something because of something that has happened

FOR MORE INFORMATION

BOOKS

Jorgensen, Katrina. *No Egg On Your Face!: Easy and Delicious Egg-Free Recipes for Kids with Allergies.* North Mankato, MN: Capstone Press, 2017.

Potts, Francesca. *All About Allergies.* Minneapolis, MN: Super Sandcastle, 2018.

WEBSITES

Food Allergies
kidshealth.org/en/kids/food-allergies.html
Read all about how the immune system works and why allergies happen.

Living with Food Allergies
www.kidswithfoodallergies.org/page/living-with-food-allergies.aspx
Find out how to stay safe when living with food allergies.

INDEX